FADGE FARLS
and
OVEN POTS

Glens of Antrim Traditional Breads
their history and recipes

Some bakers past and present
with
Helen McAlister
and
Fionnuala Carragher

Stook of Corn (Oats)

© Published by **Feís na nGleann**, 2005
Printed by Impact Printing, Ballycastle

ISBN O-948154-57-8

FADGE FARLS AND OVEN POTS

The bakers in this book are all living in the Glens of Antrim area. Our traditional breads do not use yeast as a raising agent but 'bread soda' (sodium bicarbonate), hence the term 'soda bread'. The bread rises during the cooking process. These breads have been baked for years and continue to be made although they are now cooked on modern equipment. Electric frying pans replace the 'griddle' and cookers the 'oven pots' and 'open hearth'. Some people use ingredients like yoghurt and flours with raising agents incorporated in them. Herbs, sun dried tomatoes or other dried fruit like cranberries can be used instead of the raisins or sultanas given in the recipes. 'Fadge' (potato bread) can be made with gluten free flour without any special additives. Dairy free products can be used.

Although weights and measurements are given, many of the bakers do not normally measure out their ingredients, they know by the look of the mixture in the bowl how much milk or flour is needed and use handfuls, slices and spoonfuls as well as just pouring from the bag. So the amounts in the recipes are what suit that baker's family needs. They are very personal. Each baker explains about her own baking and how she does things.

There is a very interesting insight into the history of food in the life of the Glens by Fionnuala Carragher of the Folk Museum at Cultra. Traditional bread is not just Wheaten Bread, it was not the main bread made here. You will also find 'soda bread' with fruit, treacle and caraway versions. Bread is made from oats, barley, 'yellow meal' (maize) and potatoes along with the wheat flour.

Thanks to the bakers and all those who have contributed and helped, this book is a big celebration of our traditional Glens bread-making through recipes and lore.

ADMIRE IT AND ENJOY THE WARMTH, SMELL AND TASTE OF YOUR OWN NEWLY BAKED BREAD!

INDEX

Fadge Farls and Oven Pots 3

History 6

Ingredients/Alternatives 12

Hints on Bread Making/problems 13

Round the Hearth 17

Stories   Rose Emerson 29

Flour Lore 33

Cooking Lore 47

Grist It 55

Cushendun   by Louis MacNeice 56

Bakers   *These are featured alphabetically*

Apple Fadge   Angela Jamison 31

Barley Meal Farls   Dora McCurdy 43

Carvi Bread   Anne Emerson 27

Clootie Dumpling   Memie McKeegan 46

Fadge Farls   Angela Jamison 31

Fadge Scones   Anna Douthart 19

Fruit Soda Farls   Memie McKeegan 46

Fruit Oven Scone   Anne Emerson 27

                      Peggy McNeill 49

                      Memie McKeegan (ordinary milk) 45

Oatcake	Helen McAlister	37
Oaten Fadge	Anna Douthart	19
Oaten Pancakes	Tessie O'Neill	51
Pancakes	Tessie O'Neill	51
Plain Oven Scone	Peggy McNeill	49
Potato Bread	*see Fadge, Oaten Fadge, Apple Fadge*	
Slims	Anna Douthart	23
Soda Farls	Pat Dennis (yoghurt)	15
	Teresa Duffin (ordinary milk)	25
	Anna Douthart	20
	Angela Jamison	32
Tea Scones	Mrs Danny Arthur (ordinary milk)	35
	Pat Dennis (yoghurt)	16
Treacle Farls	Anna Douthart	21
Treacle Oven	Peggy McNeill	49
	Marie Poland	53
Treacle Scones	Mrs Danny Arthur	35
Wheaten Farls	Annie McAllister	39
Wheaten (Oven)	Annie McAllister	39
	Margaret McAllister	41
	Tessie O'Neill (no weighing)	54
Yellow Meal Farls	Angela Jamison	32

LIST OF GLENS OF ANTRIM – Traditional bread in the local scene.

By *Fionnuala Carragher, Ulster Folk & Transport Museum, Cultra, Co Down.*

The foods which ordinary Glens people ate, a couple of centuries ago, were limited to what was available locally and to the foodstuffs which they had preserved or stored at home.

Free to those who had the opportunity to obtain it was wild game from the fields and hillsides. Rivers, streams, estuaries and small mountain loughs were fished, mostly for trout and salmon. The reputation, good or bad, of the principal fishing rivers and streams would be widely known.

Along the Co Antrim coastline there were many small fishing places and ports. Several Glens seaside settlements were originally fishing villages, often situated at the mouth of a salmon river. A wide range of fish was caught from inland coastal waters, as were crabs and lobsters. Fishing was usually a part-time, seasonal occupation because most fishermen were also farmers or had other employment.

The seashore provided shellfish and seaweed, which was cut from the rocks at low tide, collected and used as a fertilizer for the potato 'rigs', a type of 'raised bed' of upturned sods, elsewhere called 'lazy beds'. Alternatively, as was once common during the 19th century, it was burnt into ashes to produce kelp, a source of soda and iodine.

The seaweed duilse or dulse was popular and this feathery dark purple seaweed was gathered and munched raw as a snack or kept as a 'kitchen' or relish for a dish of boiled potatoes. Dulse may still be obtained today as a seaside treat and both old and young alike enjoy it. At the turn of the last century, fish for many families on a limited income was fresh herring in summer, with smoked and salted herring over the winter months. Ling (a fish similar to cod) was another staple food; it was bought dried and salted and soaked for several hours in water before it could be cooked. Fish was a food eaten on fast days so a weekly demand for fish remained steady well into the middle of the 20th century.

MEAT AND POULTRY

Livestock kept on farms included cattle, pigs and sheep. Horses were kept for work and they were also raised for sale. Cattle provided both milk and beef. Young cattle were often raised for sale to cattle dealers from and for export to Scotland and England. Pigs provided a variety of foods in the form of bacon, cured hams, gammon and salted pork. When a pig was killed on a farm, its soft innards were used up in a variety of methods; they went into hashes with plenty of seasoning or perhaps just pan fried in kitchen fat, together with onions and potatoes.

Sheep were raised for their wool but also for their mutton. Unlike today, one recognizable choice for a dinner dish could be a cooked pig's or sheep's head or maybe just a supper dish of pig's trotters. Lamb could be expensive, while a well-flavoured joint of mountain raised mutton was a cheaper option. Mutton is the traditional meat used in an 'Irish Stew', the famous farmhouse stew of meat, sliced potatoes, onions layered and slowly cooked together in one pot.

Meat usually meant bacon, salt pork, ham, poultry and several jointed 'cuts' of beef. 'Butcher's meat' invariably meant a joint of beef or mutton. However, the butcher's counter also supplied the cheaper cuts of pork and a selection of offal.

Some farmers also kept a few goats; they were mostly valued for their milk, which was often given as a drink to young children and as a health drink to tourists. (Goat's milk has a high fat content and it is easy to digest.)

The keeping of hens was commonplace and some farmers also kept a few geese and turkeys. There was a regular demand for chickens and eggs. Geese and turkeys were mostly raised for the Christmas market.

FRUIT, VEGETABLES AND CEREALS

A variety of both native and exotic fruit and vegetables was grown in the private enclosed kitchen gardens of the gentry. Farm garden patches supplied a long established range of vegetables including potatoes, cabbages, onions, scallions, beet and leeks. In addition, some herbs (parsley, mint and thyme), several stands of rhubarb, currant bushes and a few apple and pear trees were to be found around many farms and smaller holdings. Farmers would sell or give away surplus vegetables to relatives, friends and their immediate neighbours. Soft fruit was often made into jam for winter use or into fruit fools as a summer treat. Apples and pears were eaten raw or used in a range of dishes and desserts.

Potatoes were an important field crop. Over the decades several varieties of potato were cultivated. Cabbages were widely grown as a field crop alongside potatoes. Oats were the dominant cereal crop and oats were used both for human and animal consumption. Oatmeal was the chief ingredient found in many traditional dishes, such as porridge. For centuries, 'griddle' baked 'oatcake' was the traditional household bread.

Barley or 'bere' was grown but its cultivation went into a general decline throughout Ireland towards the end of the 19th century. Barley bread was known from medieval times (and earlier), but since bread made wholly from barley flour is dense and dark coloured, later recipes for barley bread contain a mixture of finer wheat flour. Pearl barley was used to thicken stews and broths. By the early 1900s the barley harvest was mainly reserved for use (as malt) in whiskey distilleries. Barley is a hardy and reliable cereal; during the 19th century it was grown on Rathlin Island, both for domestic use and as an exchange or cash crop.

DAIRY PRODUCE

Farmhouse made butter could be made either from whole milk or from cream skimmed from the whole milk. By the early 19th century seemingly very little cheese was made nor was it a regular part of the ordinary diet.

Earlier fragmented traditions of localised domestic cheese making existed in Co Antrim and a commercial skimmed milk hard cheese was produced in the Carrickfergus district during the 18th century. Simpler traditions of cottage style cheese making and perhaps some of the older sour milk and butter preparations may have lingered on in individual households only to disappear over time.

FAIRS AND MARKETS

Produce from farms was mostly sold in regular markets and fairs. Small local markets were often a once or twice weekly affair, while fairs were held in the larger towns about three or four times a year. Markets in smaller towns and villages were not always well attended but larger towns hosted successful events. The 'Lammas Fair' in Ballycastle is a celebrated example of a successful fair which continues onto the present day. Basic market staples included potatoes, oatmeal, butter, buttermilk, sweet milk, poultry and eggs.

At times, individual hawkers and dealers would have their own established rounds for particular foods, such as fish. By the early decades of the 20th century there were established rounds for sweet milk, egg collection, shop bread, sweet buns, and cakes. Large towns could boast a range of specialised food shops (such as a home bakery), while most villages had at least one general village shop.

By the end of the 19th century tea was an immensely popular drink. Coffee was a familiar drink but one which was commonly only offered in hotels and boarding houses. Water, milk and buttermilk were ordinary everyday drinks. Porter, whiskey and other spirits were popular alcoholic drinks and they were available from a large range of public houses and (in later decades), the new resort hotels catering for travellers and tourists. (However, Temperance reformers discouraged the drinking of alcohol.) Some illicit 'poitín' (homemade whiskey) was produced in stills but well hidden from the eyes of the law.

BREADS AND COOKING

As in other Irish country places during the 20th century, the Glens had a strong home baking tradition. This domestic tradition had its lineage in the making of the flat unleavened 'oatcake' bread on a griddle plate over the turf fire. They were made into a round, and then quartered to make 'farls'. ('Farl' comes from an old English word for a quarter.) Oatcake was also hardened on a wrought iron stand or wooden bread stick support in front of the fire. (Oatmeal was also commonly made into porridge.)

Baking soda (bicarbonate of soda) as a cheap and readily available raising agent was gradually introduced to home bakers from the 1830s onwards and its adoption encouraged the baking of a wider range of breads and tea breads. For 'soda bread', the baking soda is mixed with buttermilk and flour to make up bread dough, formed into a round and the top marked with a cross to ensure even baking.

The 19th century also saw the increased importation of the finer and softer imported American (wheat) flour into Ireland; it was of a quality which was very suitable for light textured 'soda bread' and cake making. Ingredients used to enrich breads, scones and cakes included: eggs, fat (butter or lard), dried fruit, sugar and spices. However, there are a few baking ingredients which were once popular and are no longer very common purchases, such as yellow or Indian meal, dark sticky treacle and aromatic caraway seeds.

Cooking methods were plain and straightforward. Cookery was done over an open fire. An iron 'crane' was fitted into the hearth opening and from its high cross arm, a long adjustable 'pot hook' or chain, was fitted from which pots, 'griddles' and kettles could be hung. Most rural kitchens were equipped with a basic range of utensils: a 'griddle', a few cast iron pots, a straight sided 'oven pot' (in which a 'scone' or 'cake' of bread could be baked), a 'gridiron' (grill), frying pans, a few trivets (pot/kettle stand on three low feet), and several dishes and serving implements.

Boiling, frying and baking dominated cookery. Dripping and lard were the usual fats for frying. Salt was the regular seasoning. Potatoes were mostly served boiled with or without their skins with salt and butter to taste. Potatoes were an ingredient to be added to broths, stews, boiled puddings and 'griddle' bread, ('fadge').

Today's modern Glens householder will most likely cook and bake in an up to date fitted kitchen with an improved range or gas or electric cooker and a variety of utensils and modern gadgets at hand.

Most of the traditional recipes do survive and they have been adapted for modern use and so may be enjoyed as well today as in the past.

Field of Potatoes

BASIC INGREDIENTS WITH ALTERNATIVES

FLOUR - Different brands of flour will require different amounts of liquid, so if an amount is specified in a recipe you may need to change it to suit your flour. Different batches of the same brand of flour may need different amounts of liquid. Damp weather can also affect this.

PLAIN FLOUR/ALL PURPOSE FLOUR - no raising agent is added.

SELF RAISING FLOUR (SR FLOUR) - A mixture of flour and raising agents usually used for cakes and scones. You may need to add extra raising agent.
.
SODA BREAD MIX - A mixture of flour and raising agents, sometimes salt, specially for making Soda Breads. There is also a Wheaten Mix.

BAKING SODA-E500 - (Sodium bicarbonate, bicarbonate of soda) or 'bread soda'. Add one level teaspoon /5ml spoon, with any extra shaken off, to a pound /450g of plain flour. Add one teaspoon of salt.

BAKING POWDER - E500 and E336 (*see below*).

BUTTERMILK – originally the liquid left when the butter solids are removed from churned milk. If this is not available, use any sour animal milk, even camel's milk worked. It should smell acid, but pleasant. Adding a teaspoonful of vinegar to your fresh milk can sour it. Add 2 tea/5ml spoons of lemon juice or vinegar to soya milk. Plain (unflavoured) yoghurt, with milk or water added can be used. (See Pat Dennis's recipes.) A quarter or half of buttermilk and three quarters or half of sweet milk makes a light bread. (See Memie McKeegan's Farl recipes.)

FRESH MILK - called 'sweet milk' locally.
Bread can be made using 'sweet milk' and cream of tartar, E336 (Potassium hydrogen tartrate). (See Teresa Duffin's recipe. Memie McKeegan's Oven Pot Scone, Tessie's Pancakes and Mrs Danny Arthur's scones use 'sweet milk'.)

HINTS ON BREADMAKING/problems

If using baking soda, crush all lumps in it thoroughly or use a fine sieve, otherwise there will be **brown stains** in the baked bread.

Use fresh flour. Use up the flour as quickly as possible after the bag is opened.

The best bread will be made when you don't have to add extra liquid to the initial mix, so change the amount the next time. The mixture should form one large softish ball, not wet or firm, leaving little on the sides of the bowl. If the **mixture** is slightly **wet**, add a little flour at a time from a sieve, until it all comes together. If the mixture is **too wet** to handle without adding a lot more flour, just scrape it into a greased and floured tin and bake in the oven. (See Margaret McAllister's Cottage Wheaten Loaf and Marie Poland's Fruit Treacle.)

On a floured surface, using a sieve, flour the mixture so the flour is absorbed into the mixture as a skin and does not coat it. Gently bring the edges, once, towards the middle, roll into a ball, turn it over and shape it for your particular bread. It should become a spongy workable dough. Handle and flour it only enough to be able to shape it.

If the dough is **not elasticy** or spongy then your flour has not enough raising agent.

Too firm/dry dough will give the cooked bread a **dense texture**.

Bread is baked if it has risen, sounds hollow when tapped on the base, shrinks from the sides of the tin or if a skewer put into the middle of it comes out clean. If bread is **too crumbly** when cooked and cut, it has too much fat in it. 'Soft' margarine amounts may need reduced. It is best eaten fresh, within a couple of days.

Pat Dennis

Pat Dennis was born and still lives in Coolnagoppagh (Corner of the Dockens), near Ballycastle. She bakes Soda Farls and Slims on the griddle and Fruit and Wheaten Tea Scones in the oven. As friends who wanted her recipes could not get buttermilk, she started using yoghurt in her baking. Jams and chutneys are her main cooking interest.

SODA BREAD FARLS - YOGHURT

350g (14oz) **plain flour**
1 level tea/5ml spoon of well crushed **bicarbonate of soda**
2.5ml/½ teaspoon **salt**
Approx 150ml (6 fluid ounces) **yoghurt**, mixed with
50ml (2 fluid ounces) **cold water**

NB: Use either the amounts in brackets together or the amounts outside the brackets, as they are not equivalent amounts.

1. Sieve all the ingredients together into a large bowl.
2. Make a well in the centre of the flour, pour in half the liquid, stirring from the centre.
3. Keep adding the liquid until the dough becomes elastic but not sticky.
4. Turn the dough out on to a lightly floured table, sprinkle with flour and knead until smooth.
5. Roll out or pat gently until the dough is approx 2 cms / ¾" thick.
6.. Cut the round into four and bake on a hot griddle.

NB: The griddle is hot enough to cook on, when a little flour sprinkled on it goes a beige colour.

7. Turn the Farls when they have risen and there is a skin on top and the sides are no longer sticky. You will know they are completely cooked if they sound hollow when tapped. Pat likes to brown the sides, when the Farls are cooked, by putting them up standing on their sides on the hot griddle.

Pat usually does this bread without measurements.

SODA BREAD SCONES

(Try experimenting with flavoured yoghurts)

350g (14oz) **plain flour**
¾ level tea/¾ 5ml spoon of **bicarbonate of soda**
½ tea/2.5ml spoon **salt**
½ tea/2.5ml spoon **cream of tartar**
1 **egg**
50g/2oz **margarine**
1 dessert/10ml spoon **caster sugar**
Approx 150ml (6 fluid oz) **yoghurt** mixed with
50ml (2 fluid oz) of **cold water**

NB: Use either the amounts in brackets together or the amounts outside the brackets, as they are not equivalent amounts.

1. Sieve all the dry ingredients into a large bowl.
2. Rub in the margarine.
3. Make a well in the centre; drop in the egg.
4. Add the liquid gradually, stirring from the centre, until the mixture is the consistency of soft spongy dough.
5. Turn on to a floured board, sprinkle with flour and knead lightly.
6. Roll out until the round is approx 2cms/¾" thick.
7. Cut into round scones with a cutter or glass.
8. Place scones on a lightly floured baking tray.
9. Brush lightly with a little yolk of egg or some milk.
10. Bake for approx 10 minutes until well-risen and golden brown.
11. Cool on a wire tray.

Pat does not need to measure the ingredients for her baking.

ROUND THE HEARTH

The cover shows an **open hearth**. The upright of the **crane** is on the left. It pivoted, so the arm swung over or away from the fire. One hook of the S shaped **crook** goes into the **links** (chain), the other holds the jointed curved **bools**, which here are hooked into the handles of an empty **griddle**. Flat breads like Pat's **farls,** or **pancakes, oatcake, fadge** and **slims** were cooked on these.

Another pot hangs from a different style of **crook**, which was normally used for heavier pots. The **crook** could be raised or lowered over the heat by moving it up or down in the **links**. The smallest round-bottomed pot was used for cooking porridge; the largest 18 gallons/82 litres was used to boil potatoes for pigs.

A round **pot stand** for the kettle to rest on, is to the right of the **griddle**.

On the left hang **bellows**. Unless company was in, it was more normal for a woman to flap her apron to cause a draught to get the fire going than to use bellows. Lying on the hearth are **tongs**, which were used to place pieces of turf on to the fire.

At the bottom are an **oven pot** holding an **oven pot scone** and a **griddle** with **fadge farls**. These items give the book its title.

A **crook staff** for working with sheep was made by boiling a length of hazel wood in the largest pot, and one end bent round pegs on a wooden board.

Booly legged: a person who had bowlegs that seemed to spring up and down as they walked. **Booled:** means an item stretched up over something.

Most of the photographs in this book were taken between 2003 and 2005.

Anna Douthart

Anna Douthart lives in Glenshesk. She makes Soda and Treacle Farls, Plain and Fruit Slims, Fadge, Oaten Fadge and Pancakes on the griddle, and Fruit Loaf in the oven. Anna won a Feis medal when she entered Wheaten Bread. In the photograph she is preparing Fadge. She bakes for neighbours.

FADGE AND OATEN FADGE

Freshly boiled **potatoes**   Hot griddle
Salt to your own taste
½ teacup fine **oatmeal** (for Oaten Fadge)
Plain flour or brown rice flour for gluten free Fadge

1. Mash the potatoes while they are hot and add the salt. (For Oaten Fadge, add the oats.) If they are too hot to handle, mix in flour until you can handle the potatoes safely and transfer them to a floured working surface.

2. Roll into a thick roll with your hands. Cut this into lengths about ¼"/5mm to ½"/15mm thick, one for each scone. Work a little more flour into each scone gradually with your hands until it is no longer sticky to touch. Put four fork marks in each scone top, to let the steam out.

3. Check the griddle is hot enough. If you sprinkle a little flour on its surface, it should go dark brown, but not burn. Put the Fadge on the griddle at this stage.

4. Turn when a skin forms on top. It should take about 2-3 minutes each side.

6-8 medium sized potatoes will make 6-8 scones.

 GENERAL HINTS- Mash the potatoes when they are hot or they will go lumpy. If they are very dry add a little milk or butter at this stage. If you add too much flour the mixture will have cracks and break up, just add enough until the mixture is no longer sticky. Add it to the individual Scones like Anna does, or to all the potatoes, like Angela Jamison does.

SODA FARLS

10oz/300g **self raising flour**
½pt/300ml **buttermilk** approximately

1. Put griddle or electric skillet to medium hot setting.

2. In a bowl gradually mix the buttermilk into the flour until you have a firmish dough. Turn out on a floured board and flour, kneading the mixture until smooth.

3. Roll out to 10"/250mm diameter and approx ½" thick /15mm. Cut into four Farls (quarters). Put on to a medium-hot floured griddle.

NB: To check for the right temperature – flour put on the griddle should turn medium brown quickly.

4. Leave for approximately 5 minutes. Farls should begin to form a skin on the top and have risen slightly before turning over. When ready, turn and cook for another five minutes.

5. Remove from the griddle and put on a cooler tray and cover with a dry tea towel until the bread is cold.

Makes approximately four Sodas.

For all her breads Anna pours flour into the bowl and knows just the right amount of liquid to add.

For Anna's recipes on this and the following pages, if you use plain flour, add 1 level teaspoon/5ml spoon of baking soda and salt to 1lb/450g flour.

TREACLE SODAS

10oz/300g **self raising flour**
2 dessert/10ml spoons **treacle**
½ pint/300ml **buttermilk** approx

1. Set griddle or electric skillet to medium heat.

2. In a bowl, rub the treacle into the dry flour with the hands until the mixture resembles breadcrumbs.

3. Mix in the buttermilk until it becomes a firmish dough and flour while kneading on a floured board.

4. Roll out to approx ½"/15mm thick and 175-200mm /7"to 8" diameter.

5. Cut into quarters and put on a medium-hot floured griddle.

NB: The flour on the griddle should turn a light golden brown quickly when the griddle is hot enough to start cooking.

6. Cook for about 5 minutes. Check that a skin has formed on top and that the bread has risen; then it is ready to turn over. Cook for a further five minutes on the other side.

7. Remove from the griddle, put on a cooler tray and cover with a tea towel until cold.

Makes approximately four Sodas.

Barrel Churn

SLIMS

Plain and Fruit Slims   Medium hot griddle

10oz/300g **self raising flour**
1 dessert/10ml spoon **syrup**
1oz/25g **margarine**
1oz/25g **sugar**
1 **egg** (medium)
½pt/300ml **buttermilk** approx

1. Add syrup and margarine to the dry flour in a bowl and rub together until it resembles breadcrumbs.
2. Add sugar and a handful of raisins, if making Fruit Slims.
3. Mix together.
4. Add the egg and enough buttermilk until the dough is firm.
5. Put on to a floured board and sprinkle with flour and work lightly.
6. Roll out to ¼" thick /5mm and cut with a round cutter or cut into triangles.
7. Cook on a medium-hot floured griddle. You will know it is hot enough to commence baking when the flour turns a medium brown quickly.
8. Turn after about 2/3 minutes, when the top has a skin and the bread has risen slightly.

Makes approx twelve Slims.

Teresa Duffin

Teresa was born in Coleraine and now lives on the slopes above Glenravel. Her mother came from Carnlough, where Teresa's grandfather worked as a gamekeeper for the Turnly family. Like her mother, Teresa uses ordinary milk instead of buttermilk. She says that this gives a different flavour to the bread. Teresa bakes Soda Farls, Pancakes and Scones, and makes jams.

SODA FARLS – WITHOUT BUTTERMILK

Set electric pan to 240°C/460°F

12oz/350g **soda bread flour** *or*
same amount of **plain flour** with a level tea/5ml spoon of **baking soda** and
a level tea/5ml spoon of **salt** added
1 tea/5ml spoon **cream of tartar**
½ pt/300ml fresh **milk** approx

1. In a bowl, use a metal spoon to bring all the ingredients together, as it will mix everything more quickly than a wooden spoon. This will be soft sticky dough.

2. Put out on a floured board; dust the mixture lightly with flour. Shape by hand into a round and flatten to about ½"/5mm, again as quickly as possible. Cut into four Farls and place on hot griddle.

NB: A little flour sprinkled on the hot surface will turn golden and when it darkens further (not burning) it is time to put the bread on.

3. Cook 5 minutes approximately each side. It is ready to turn over when it has risen and the sides spring out if you touch them with your thumb or finger.

The bread softens as it cools. Store in an airtight container.

Anne Emerson

Anne came from Co Monaghan. She bakes Soda Farls, Pancakes, Oven Wheaten, Currant and Treacle in the oven. Anne adds an egg to all her bread and finds this keeps it fresh for longer. To make good bread, she feels you need to use fresh flour, so use up the flour soon after you open the bag. Her mother-in-law Rose Emerson was also a keen baker.

OVEN POT FRUIT SODA AND CARVI BREAD

1lb/450g **plain flour**
1 level tea/5ml spoon of crushed **baking powder**
1 level tea/5ml spoon **salt**
1 medium/2oz/50g **egg**, beaten lightly
2oz/50g **margarine**/a lump
2oz/50g/2 dessertspoons **sugar**
4oz/100g/a few handfuls **dried fruit**
16fl oz/ ⅔ pint/400ml **buttermilk** approx
For Carvi Bread add 2 tea/5 ml spoons of **caraway seed**

Anne does not need to weigh/measure her flour and buttermilk when she bakes.

1. Set the oven to Gas Mark 6/200°C/400°F. Grease and flour the oven pot or casserole, including the lid and heat it in the oven.

2. Rub the margarine well into the flour and sugar and baking soda, in a bowl. Add the fruit.

3. Make a hole in the middle of the mixture and add the buttermilk and egg, mixing in the one direction with a wooden spoon to a spongy dough, not wet or firm.

4. On a flat surface, shape and flour the bread and flatten by hand to fit the oven pot. Place it in the pot and cut a cross in the surface and lightly prick it.

5. Put at the top of a hot oven. Now reduce the heat to Gas Mark 4/180°C/350°F for 55 min – 1 hour, until risen. When it is cooked it should sound hollow and when a skewer is put into it, it should come out clean. Eat fresh.

Rose Emerson

Rose Emerson was a well-known baker. Soda Farls were made daily, a ten stone bag/6.4 kg of 'white flour' only did a fortnight.   She also cooked most of the breads mentioned in the book. Her house was a place to 'céilí', with stories. If you called in and got up to go without even taking tea or coffee, you were told that you had had a 'dry céilí'. The road to her house became locally known as Rosie's Road.

LOCAL LORE: Stories by Rose Emerson

Hungry Grass

Part of Layde, Cushendall has 'Hungry Grass'. It was said that if you walked over particular pieces of ground, you got a feeling of weakness and severe pain in your stomach. If you didn't get off it quickly you would die. Some people say that it is found where grass grows on the site of a derelict famine house.

Turf

Turf spoke once and said,

> "If you want to be my friend,
> Put me up upon my end."

To get turf to burn on the hearth, you set it up in a wigwam shape, so the air got underneath and it burned.

Loughareema – between Glendun and Ballycastle

A young woman had taken hot soda bread, up to the people at the 'turf cutting', but decided to rest before heading home. While she was sitting beside Loughareema, an enormous bull came out of the water and lay down with his head on her lap. The poor girl didn't know what was going to happen to her when he woke up. Carefully she undid her apron and then slipped away as quietly as she could, so as not to waken him. Then she took to her heels and ran as fast as she could. When she reached the safety of the hills, she rested. Down in the hollow she could hear the bull roaring.

In the past, the emptying lake made a roaring sound.

Angela Jamison

Angela Jamison was born and lives in Glenariff. She learned her bread making skills from her grandmother who is pictured above with Angela's own mother. Angela makes Soda Farls, Treacle Farls, Slims, Pancakes, Fadge and Scones.

Angela can assess when the cooking surface is at the correct temperature by holding her palm at a distance above it.

FADGE FARLS

1lb (400g) **cooked potatoes**, mashed while hot and salted and peppered to your taste
2oz (50g) **plain flour**
or
2oz (50g) **brown rice flour** for gluten free Fadge

NB: Either use the measurements outside the brackets or those inside the brackets; do not mix them.

1. Mix the ingredients together well.

2. Divide the mixture into two.

3. Shape each into a circle and roll the mixture on a floured surface, until it is about ¼"/5mm thick.

4. Cut each circle into four sections.

5. Bake on a hot slightly oiled griddle (200ºC), until there is a brown skin underneath.

6. Turn and cook, checking the underside again.

This makes eight Farls.

For APPLE FADGE, put **cooked apple** on the uncooked Farls, fold over and press edges together. Cook as above, eat hot.

YELLOW MEAL FARLS

5oz/125g **polenta/maize flour**
1lb/475g **soda bread flour**
or same amount **plain flour** with 1 tea/5ml spoon each of crushed **baking soda** and **salt**
18fl oz/500ml **buttermilk** approximately * see below

Makes 8 Farls

1. Mix the dry ingredients together, in a bowl.
2. Add enough buttermilk so the dough is not sticky.
3. Transfer to a floured surface.
4. Divide the mixture into two.
5. Shape each bit into a circle, flouring as needed, and roll into a circle about ½"/15mm thick.
6. Cut into four.
7. Cook on a slightly greased griddle, preheated to 400ºF/200ºC, for 10 minutes. The sides of the Farl will show it has risen and will be firm and no longer sticky to the touch.
8. Turn. Reduce the temperature to 300ºF/150ºC .
9. Cook a further 10 minutes.

The bread should not be doughy. You need to cook the Farls immediately after they are prepared otherwise the mixture becomes stringy.

* Granny's secret ingredient for perfect Farls.
Add a teaspoon of **Golden Syrup** when you are adding the buttermilk, to any type of Soda Farl. For PLAIN FARLS use 1lb5oz/600g **flour.**

FLOUR LORE

"YELLOW MEAL was brought in as famine relief, at the time of the Potato Famine, in the 1840s. You didn't tell people that you were eating bread made from it, although it tasted nice. You could make porridge from it, like oatmeal porridge."
"The flour was known as Golden Drop."
"Maize was fed to animals. We used the same meal as was fed to the cows, but only baked with it when the bag was first opened."

"Emigrants, on the boats, took Oatcake."
The OATS, known as corn, were grown locally and taken to the mill nearby, to be ground into meal.
"I remember seeing people going to the mill, in Glenane."

BARLEY was grown and used for baking bread, on Rathlin.
"There was a race to see who would be the first person to grind the barley once it was sheafed. If bread was made too soon after the barley was harvested, the people who ate the bread used to stagger around. This was called 'sturdied'. Barley is no longer grown on Rathlin. Barley straw was used for thatching."
We were able to source barley meal from an organic flour supplier but it only comes in 25kg/4 stone bags.

"We were snowed in near Cushendall, in the 1950s, for three weeks. I was able to cope because I had just bought a large bag of 'white flour' (WHEAT). We had hens and our own milk, so I could make bread. We kept a large bag of 'white flour' and a smaller one of 'yellow meal', beside the fire."

CARAWAY (Carum carvi) grew at Aggie McClarty's and Kane's up Layde, Cushendall.
"Caraway was ready to pick, when the hay was being cut."

Mrs Danny Arthur

Mrs. Danny Arthur (McAlister), 83, was born in Glenariff. She bakes Sweet Cakes, Tarts, Scones and Soda Farls. Her husband's name was Danny McAlister but as there are so many McAlisters in the area, he was known locally instead by his father's first name, Arthur. This told him apart from Danny Dan also Danny McAlister, but in his case his father was Dan. People with other surnames are also told apart in this way. Pat Archie instead of Pat McNeill.

SCONES

200g/8oz **self raising flour**
¼ level tea/¼ 5ml spoon **salt**
50g/2oz **margarine or butter**
50g/2oz **sugar**
50g/2oz **currants** (optional)
Fresh **milk** 125ml approx
½ tea/½ 5ml spoon **baking powder**
Set oven to 218ºC/425ºF/Gas Mark 7

1. Sieve the flour, baking powder and salt into a bowl.
2. Add the fat in small pieces to the flour.
3. Rub it in until it looks like breadcrumbs.
4. Mix in the sugar and fruit (if needed) and add the milk a tea/5ml spoon at the time, mixing well after each spoonful until the mixture all comes together and the dough leaves the bowl clean. Do not get a soft consistency. You can use your hand to do the mixing.
5. Transfer the mixture on to a floured surface, flour lightly and form it into a flat roundish shape. Roll out to about one inch or 25mm.
6. Cut with a pastry cutter or round floured drinking glass and then brush the top of each scone with milk to glaze it.
7. Bake on a greased baking tray, near the top of the oven, for about ten minutes until risen and golden brown.

Mrs Danny Arthur used to use plain flour and baking soda (about 1 tea/5ml spoon). She now prefers self raising flour.

For TREACLE SCONES add a dessert/10ml spoon of **treacle** when you start mixing the milk into the ingredients.

Helen McAlister

Helen lives in Glendun. Her mother, from Bellaghy, Co Derry, used to make Pancakes and Scones, souring the ordinary milk with vinegar if no buttermilk was available. Her father's family of McAlisters was known as the Robbies eg Alfie Robbie. Helen measures with teacups. She mainly makes oven Wheaten Bread.

OATCAKE

Preheat the oven to 180°C/350°F/Gas Mark 4.
Lightly grease two baking trays.

Melt 1oz/25g **butter** or **margarine** in
¼ pint/150ml **boiling water** and add both to a bowl with
½lb/225g **fine oatmeal** mixed with a big pinch of **salt**
and a big pinch of **baking soda**, crushed to a smooth powder.

> Stir everything together and mix well into one non-sticky ball, which
> you can shape. Work more oatmeal into it, if it is too wet.
> Cut it into two even pieces, checking that there are no airspaces and
> work each into a flattened shape on a board, lightly sprinkled with
> oatmeal. Roll out thinly to 2mm/⅛".
> Cut into rounds or eight triangles, leaving the edges rough, trimming
> them or neaten with the prongs of a fork.
> Use a knife to lift them on to the prepared trays.
> Cook on the 2nd and 3rd shelves of the oven, for about 25 minutes until
> firm and slightly coloured.
> Remove from the oven and turn them over, checking to see if any of the
> undersides are greyish or dark, as those are undercooked.
> If necessary, replace the trays in the oven, with the Oatcakes upside
> down, putting the undercooked ones on the hottest shelf. Check after a
> further five minutes, to see that they are all cooked. Don't worry if they
> curl at the edges.

Cooked Oatcake should click when clipped by your fingernail. Cool on a wire tray and
then put in an airtight container.

Mrs Anna McAllister

Mrs Anna McAllister, 78, was born in Glenmakeeran, near Ballycastle. She knows how much baking soda she needs and puts it in the palm of her hand to crush it, but uses empty margarine cartons as her measure for the flour. "Annie" bakes nearly every other day, making Soda and Wheaten Farls, Pancakes, Oven Wheaten, Currant Soda and Fadge. She bakes a Scottish Shortbread, Swiss Rolls and Carvi cake.

GRIDDLE WHEATEN BREAD

8oz/225g **wheaten meal**
4oz/125g **plain flour**
1 tea/5ml spoon **salt**
1 tea/5ml spoon well crushed **baking soda**
1 tea/5ml spoon **syrup**
1½ oz/25g **margarine**
½ pt/300ml **buttermilk** approx

1. Put the wheaten meal and plain flour into a mixing bowl. Add salt and baking soda.
2. Rub in the margarine, add syrup and finally add buttermilk. Mix to a nice pliable dough.
3. On a floured surface, roll out into a large circle about ½"/15mm thick and cut into four Farls.

NB: To test the griddle is hot enough, sprinkle a little flour over its surface. It should tint the flour.

4. Place the Farls on the griddle for approx seven minutes. They are ready to turn, if a skin has formed on top of them.
5. Cook the turned Farl a further seven minutes. If you prefer the sides of the Farl brown, set them up on their ends on the griddle, as in her photograph. Wrap them in a clean **dry** tea towel to cool. This leaves the bread softer. Serve hot or cold.

OVEN WHEATEN. Turn the mixture from the bowl directly into a 6"/15cm round floured cake tin. Smooth the surface with a heated spoon and then mark it with a cross . Bake for about thirty-five minutes at Gas Mark 6/400ºF/200ºC. When cooked the base of the tin should sound hollow when tapped. Wrap the bread in a **damp** tea towel.

Margaret McAllister

Margaret McAllister was born in Belfast, but now lives in Glenarm. Her father's family came from Cairncastle, near Larne, Co Antrim. While her Aunt Peggy in Galway, who is pictured above, gave the recipe to her, she feels it may have originated from Cairncastle. Margaret bakes Wheaten Bread and Scones.

COTTAGE WHEATEN LOAF

6oz/175g **soda bread** or **self raising flour**
1 level tea/5ml spoon **baking soda**, crushed well
12oz/325g **wheaten meal flour**
or 10oz/275g **wheaten meal** and 2oz/50g **pinhead oats**
½ tea/½ 5ml spoon **salt**
1 dessert/10ml spoon **dark brown sugar**
1oz/25g **margarine**
⅔ dessert/ ⅔ 10ml spoon **treacle**
14floz/400ml **buttermilk** approx

1. Set oven at 400°F/200°C/Gas Mark 6

2. Sieve the white flour and baking soda into a large bowl and add wheaten flour, salt and sugar.

3. Rub in the margarine. Add the buttermilk and treacle to form a loose dough.

4. Spoon into a greased and floured 2lb loaf tin and sprinkle the top with wheaten meal to give a nutty surface.

5. Bake at 400°F/200°C/Gas Mark 6 for 30 minutes, and then reduce to 325°F/160°C/Gas Mark 3 for a further 30 minutes.

6. It should feel firm and sound hollow when tapped.

NB: Proportion of flour to wheaten flour is according to taste. Pinhead oats give a coarser texture.

Mrs Dora McCurdy

Mrs Dora McCurdy, 87, is a native of Rathlin. She baked Soda and Fruit Soda Farls, Pancakes, Yellow Meal and Barley Farls. Barley Bread is the one bread in the book no longer normally made. It has a different texture to Wheaten Bread. In the oven she baked Oven Scones, either plain or fruit. Mrs McCurdy no longer bakes but supervises when her daughter is baking in her place.

BARLEY BREAD RECIPE

8oz/225g **barley meal**
6oz/175g **plain flour**
1 tea/5ml spoon **salt**
1 dessert/10ml spoon of **sugar** (optional)
¾ pint/400 ml **buttermilk** approximately
1 level tea/5ml spoon **baking soda**

Mrs McCurdy would not normally have needed to weigh her ingredients.

1. Put all the dry ingredients into a bowl and mix together.

2. Add in the buttermilk and mix to a not wet dough consistency.

3. Turn out the dough on to a floured board, flour lightly and knead well.

4. Roll out the dough and cut into four squares about ½"/15mm in thickness.

5. Bake on the hot griddle turning over once or twice.

The bread is cooked when you are able to touch it and it feels firm. It can be eaten straight from the griddle, but it is easier to cut when allowed to cool.

NB: Instead of barley meal, barley flakes can be made into flour in a coffee grinder or food processor.

Memie McKeegan

Memie, née ONeill, lives in Glendun. She has inherited her mother Tessie's baking skills, cooking Soda, Fruit and Wheaten Farls about twice a week followed by Pancakes on the still hot griddle. An Oven Pot Scone would be a weekly bake. Memie has done baking demonstrations and did one for the 2004 Feis Centenary celebrations.

RICH OVEN POT SCONE

Preheat a greased and floured 8"/20cm diameter ovenproof casserole.

1¼ lbs/550g **self raising flour**
or 1¼lbs/550g **plain flour** (with ½ teaspoon/½ 5ml spoon of **bicarbonate of soda** and
1 tea/5ml spoon of **baking powder**)
8oz/200g **sugar**
¼tea/¼ 5ml spoon **salt**
12oz/325g **mixed fruit**
2 **eggs** (medium) lightly beaten
2oz/50g melted **butter**
Fresh **milk** to mix, 1¼ pts/25fl oz/700ml approx

Memie would normally just put unweighed ingredients into the bowl.

1. Mix all the dry ingredients together.
2. Add the lightly beaten eggs.
3. Mix in the melted butter.
4. Add sufficient milk to form a light dough.
5. Transfer to a floured surface, and dust lightly with flour. Press the floured dough into a preheated pot or first roll it out very lightly to approx 2"/5cms thick and then add the mixture to a hot well greased floured pot.
6. Cover with a lid.
7. Bake at 420°F/220°C/Gas Mark 7 for about 75 minutes, in the middle of the oven.

It is cooked when it sounds hollow if the surface is knocked.

NB: An oven proof, if possible iron pot with a lid, is desirable for baking this Scone.

GRIDDLE FRUIT SODA BREAD (FARLS)

Electric Griddle to 350°F/180°C

1lb/450g **soda bread flour**
or 1lb/450g **plain flour** with1 level tea/5ml spoon **bicarbonate of soda**
½ tea spoon or ½ 5ml spoon **salt**
4oz/100g **margarine** or **butter**
3oz/75g **sugar**
4oz/100g **sultanas** normally measured in handfuls
Approx 10fl oz/300ml **buttermilk** with 10fl oz/250ml fresh **milk**

1. Rub the margarine/ butter into the flour. Add sugar and fruit.
2. Mix to a fairly soft dough with the milk mixture.
3. On a floured surface, flour and knead lightly to form a round about ¼"/5mm thick. Cut into diamonds or other shapes with a cutter.
4. Put on a hot griddle

NB: Sprinkle flour on the heated griddle, if it lightly colours it is ready to cook on. If it turns brown, it is too hot.

5. Cook until there is a skin on top of the Farl. You can check the underneath has cooked, turn and cook for another ten minutes.

*Memie's grandmother's secret ingredient for plain Soda Farls was a **teaspoonful of sugar.***

CLOOTIE DUMPLING: Memie says that a sweeter version of her Oven Pot Scone with 2 table/15ml spoons of **treacle** and some **dates** can be boiled in a greased and floured cloth for about two of hours. When cooked it has an outer skin and sounds hollow when tapped. Cut it into slices, which can be fried on the pan.

COOKING LORE

"For cooking, turf was used on the 'open hearth', in preference to coal, as the coal embers died and went cold; with turf you could add more and it gave a constant heat."

"The 'oven pot' had a flat lid, so you could put some turf embers on top of it for all round heat. Some parts of the Glens talk of turf, others peat."

"On Rathlin they had no peat. On one part of the island, when they used the 'oven pot' etc, they burned the dry stalks of the beans grown as animal feed or used ragwort, now classified as toxic. Others cut 'the sod', the fibrous top layer made by the roots of gorse or heather, which was cut and dried like peat. Later peat came over by boat."

"A goose wing from the Christmas bird was used to brush the flour off the working surface or the excess flour off the cooked bread."

"As well as bread, fruit tarts were cooked in the 'oven pot'. To check when it was hot enough to cook in it, a little flour sprinkled on the bottom turned dark brown quickly."

"When Oatcake was taken off the 'griddle' the underside was dried out against a piece of turf or pieces were set up together, like upside down Vs, at the hearth edge."

"I cooked on the 'open hearth', until the 1970s."

" 'Mealy Creeshy' was made by frying handfuls of oatmeal in hot bacon fat, until it was crisp."

"When salted fish was cooked on top of the potatoes in the 'three legged pot' it seasoned the potatoes."

Peggy McNeill

Peggy McNeill, née McAuley (Peggy Davey), 76, was born and lives in Glenane. She normally baked Soda Farls, Slims, Pancakes, Fadge and Oven Fruit Sodas. She uses soda bread flour now but found that her soda bread flour did not lift the bread enough for Yellow Meal Farls and she needed to use baking soda and plain flour instead. Peggy measures her flour with a very big spoon instead of weighing it. She mixes with a wooden spoon feeling that a metal spoon cuts the dough.

PLAIN SODA SCONE

14oz/400g **flour**
If using **plain flou**r, add 1 tea/5ml spoon each of **salt** and crushed **baking soda**
2oz/50g **sugar**
2oz/50g **margarine** or **butter**
1 **egg**
9fl oz/250ml **buttermilk** approx

The above ingredients are half of what Peggy would use. The double amount is baked in a square roasting tin.

Oven – Gas Mark 4/180ºC/350ºF

1. Grease and lightly flour a medium flattish baking tin.
2. Put the flour and sugar in a mixing bowl. Rub in the margarine until it becomes the texture of breadcrumbs. Beat the eggs and buttermilk together. Add to the other ingredients and mix to a fairly stiff dough with a wooden spoon. Try not to get the consistency too thin or soft/wet.
3. Place mixture on to a floured surface. Dust just enough flour over it until you can shape it with your hands to the size of the baking tin and lift it from the board to the tin. Press the mixture into the corners of the tin.
4. Cut surface into four. Prick each section about three times with a fork, to allow it to rise evenly. Sprinkle the surface with a little flour.
5. Bake for an hour at the top of the oven. It is baked when it has risen, the top is golden and the mixture has shrunk from the sides of the tin. You can check that it is cooked by pushing a skewer into the centre of the loaf. It should come out clean.

For FRUIT SODA, add 3oz **mixed fruit**, before adding the liquid. For TREACLE SODA, add 1 tablespoon of **treacle** into the buttermilk.

Tessie O Neill

Tessie O Neill, née McIlhatton, 90, in 2004, was born in Glenravel, but has lived in Glendun since 1940. She has baked most bread. At home her mother made Oatcake but she says that she has never made it. Her father was a shoemaker. A brother Mickey, a shepherd for the Dobbs, was known as the 'King of the Glens', and was a renowned fiddler and maker of 'poitín'. He baked, as his wife could not. Tessie's husband's family name was Ned.

SHROVE TUESDAY PANCAKES – made for all her neighbours, one of whom was Pat Archie (McNeill).

Set electric frying pan to 350°F/180°C.

1lb/450g **self raising flour**
or 1lb **plain flour** with ½ tea/½ 5ml spoon of crushed **baking soda**
or **ground almonds** and **raising agent** for a gluten free version
Pinch of **salt**
1 dessert/10ml spoon of **sugar** or **Golden Syrup**
2 **eggs** (medium) mixed with1 pint/550ml fresh **milk**
or use **buttermilk** or a mixture of **milk** and **buttermilk**
Dash of **lemon juice** (about 1 tea/5ml spoon)
2oz/50g **melted butter**

1. Put flour, salt and sugar all in a bowl (baking soda if needed) and add the milk and eggs. Mix vigorously.
2. Add the melted butter and lemon juice. Beat again, making sure the flour is well mixed. It will be a thick creamy consistency.

Tessie normally just pours an amount of flour into a bowl and knows how much liquid to add to get this consistency.

3. Try a small teaspoonful on a heated greased griddle/pan. If it is hot enough, it will only spread a little. Tessie transfers the mixture to a jug, and pours to the preferred size of Pancake on the griddle pan. Cook until bubbles rise on the pancake surface and settle again. You can loosen them from the pan as they cook. Turn and cook a further five minutes.

Makes 18-20 Pancakes, in batches. Butter and serve with sugar, jam or honey when hot.

For OATMEAL PANCAKES, add ½ teacup of fine **oatmeal** when you are weighing out the flour.

Marie Poland

Marie came from Belfast and now lives outside Glenarm. She bakes Scones, Oven Wheaten, Oven Soda and Treacle Bread. Her mother-in-law, shown in the photograph, was born near Limavady, Co Derry, but later set up home in the Braid. She continued to make Oatcake, thick and with sugar, using an ordinary range/cooker but still drying it is with a "har'nen iron", the wrought iron stand mentioned by Fionnuala Carragher. Mrs. McLaughlin died a couple of years ago at the age of 90.

TREACLE SODA BREAD

1lb/450g **soda bread flour**
1 table/15ml spoon **brown sugar**
2oz/50g **sultanas**
½ pint/300ml **buttermilk**
2 table/15ml spoons of **treacle**
1 medium **egg**

If using **plain flou**r, add a tea/5ml spoon of **baking soda** and **salt**.

1. Mix the flour, sugar and sultanas in a bowl.

2. Beat together the egg, treacle and buttermilk and then add to the dry ingredients.

3. Mix together to make soft dough. Add more buttermilk if necessary.

4. Spoon the mixture into a greased 2lb baking tin.

5. Bake in a moderate oven (400ºF/200ºC/Gas Mark 6), for about 40 minutes.

6. Turn the bread out of the tin and leave on a wire rack to cool.

TESSIE'S WHEATEN LOAF

Oven 350°F/180°C/Gas Mark 4.

1 teacup **plain flour**
1½ teacups **wheaten flour**
or 1 cup **wheaten flour** and ½ cup **bran**
a thin slice of **butter**
1 level tea/5ml spoon **baking soda** crushed
1 dessert/10ml spoon **sugar** or to taste
½ tea/½ 5ml spoon **salt**
1½ cups **buttermilk** approx

Tessie's teacup held 4½oz/125g flour/ wheaten flour; 1½ of her teacups held 12floz/350ml of buttermilk and her slice of butter was around 1oz/25g. It should work, if your cup is smaller or larger, as long as you only use one size of cup throughout.

She normally just pours the ingredients from the bag or bottle into the bowl.

1. Rub the margarine into the dry ingredients and mix with the buttermilk to form soft dough.

2. Either transfer the mixture to a greased and floured bread tin, or on a floured surface lightly flour the dough and shape for the tin. Turn into the prepared bread tin.

3. Bake in a preheated oven for about an hour until it sounds hollow when tapped.

GRIST IT

The term 'grist' came up. One person said that she knew by looking at, and feeling the mixture, how much flour to add to her Fadge.
"I grist it."

Anna McAllister knew that her griddle was hot enough to put the bread on, without needing to see if the flour had become 'tinted'. She holds her hand flat, a distance above the hot griddle and knows, by the heat sensation against her palm, when she can start cooking.
She said, "I grist it."

When Peggy McNeill flours and works the dough, she estimates that its texture is correct so she can handle it to press it into the corners of the tin without it sticking to her fingers.
"I grist it."

She said about the balance of the raising agent to flour in her soda bread flour,
"It makes good bread, they must have got the 'grist' right."

'Grist' (rhymes with wrist) is an old dialect word, which has survived here, and elsewhere. It means to gauge.

As you become used to baking, hopefully you will instinctively know what to do at the various stages of your baking. One day you too will be able to say,
"I grist it."

These verses by Louis MacNeice, dated to August/September 1939, describe a wider Glens landscape, little changed from the one you will find to day.

From Cushendun Series

Fuchsia and ragweed and the distant hills
Made as it were out of clouds and sea:
All night the bay is plashing and the moon
Marks the break of the waves.

Limestone and basalt and a whitewashed house
With passages of great stone flags
And a walled garden with plums on the wall
And a bird piping in the night.

Forgetfulness: brass lamps and copper jugs
And home-made bread and the smell of turf or flax
And the air a glove and the water lathering easy
 And convolvulus in the hedge.

Only in the dark green room beside the fire
With the curtains drawn against the winds and waves
There is a little box with a well-bred voice:
What a place to talk of War.

From **Collected Poems**, Louis MacNeice, Published by Faber.
Printed by kind permission of David Higham Associates.